Treasure Hunt

A Brother's Tale

Catie Songster

Illustrations by Abigail Louie

ISBN 979-8-89243-945-9 (paperback)
ISBN 979-8-89428-545-0 (hardcover)
ISBN 979-8-89243-946-6 (digital)

Christian Faith Publishing
832 Park Avenue
Meadville, PA 16335
www.christianfaithpublishing.com

Printed in the United States of America

To "26," Weston, and George, my three favorites.

Heartfelt thanks to Lisa Plog for spending many hours editing with me, and to Abby Louie for doing a wonderful job illustrating!

Special thanks to my loving husband and to our magnificent Maker, who puts His treasure in us (2 Corinthians 4:6–7).

Two big brothers raced by like a flash;
Straight past their brother,
they made a dash.
They yelled aloud as they went by,
"Treasure! That's what we will find!"

Little brother stood by and cried,
"Wait! You can't leave me behind!"

They stopped and said, "Together's no fun!
We are fast and want to run!"

All at once, a fancy feather caught their eye as it floated by.
"You stay here and guard this treasure! Don't follow us, don't even try!"

"Who knows," they said, "which way we'll go!
We'll search up high, and we'll search down low!
We will not rest
'til we've found the best!"

③

"Look!" one yelled. "Is *that* our treasure?
See…a tall and towering tree!
Could it be? What could be better?"

4

"Hurray! Let's go!" they called out
and dashed over across the ground.

They climbed up, they climbed down,
they climbed over and all around!
Little brother followed but made no sound.

6

One stopped and said, "What a ton of fun!
But wait…is *this* the very best one?"

All at once, a hunting hawk
caught their eye as it soared on by.
"Will she lead us to
better treasure?"
"Follow her! It's worth a try!"

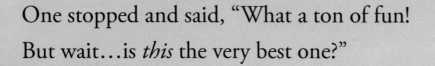

7

"Who knows," they said,
"which way we'll go!"

8

"We'll search up high, and we'll search down low!

We will not rest

'til we've found the best!"

"Look!" one yelled. "Is *that* our treasure?
See…a big and bumpy boulder!
Could it be? What could be better?"

"Yay! Let's *go*!" they called out
and dashed over across the ground.

They jumped up, they jumped down,
they jumped over and all around!
Little brother followed but made no sound.

One stopped and said, "What a ton of fun!
But wait…is *this* the very best one?"

11

All at once, a crazy cricket caught their eye as it whizzed on by.

"Will he lead us to better treasure?"

"Follow him! It's worth a try!"

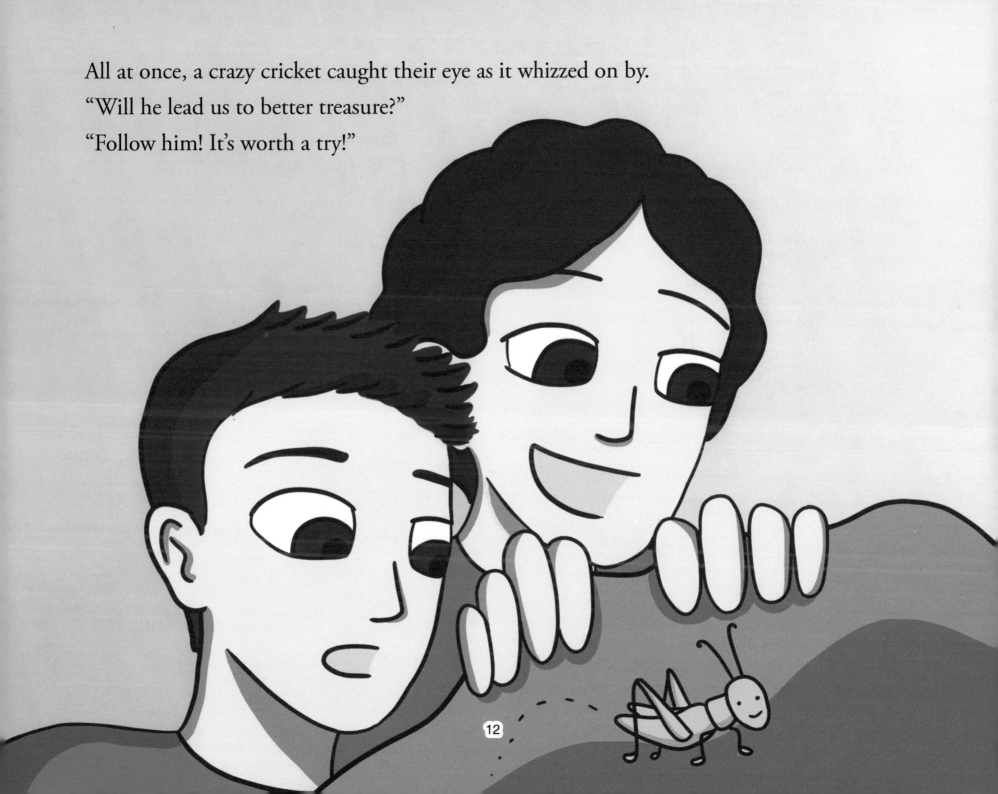

"Who knows," they said, "which way we'll go!
We'll search up high, and we'll search down low!"
We will not rest
'til we've found the best!"

13

"Look!" one yelled. "Is *that* our treasure?
See…a shallow, sparkling stream!
Could it be? What could be better?"

"Great! Let's *go*!" they called out and dashed over across the ground.
They splashed up, they splashed down, they splashed over and all around!
Little brother followed but made no sound.

One stopped and said, "What a ton of fun!
But wait…is *this* the very best one?"

All at once, a brilliant butterfly caught their eye as she fluttered by.

"Will she lead us to better treasure?"

"Follow her! It's worth a try!"

"Who knows," they said, "which way we'll go!
We'll search up high, and we'll search down low!
We will not rest
'til we've found the best!"

17

"Look!" one yelled. "Is *that* our treasure?
See…a high and humongous hill!
Could it be? What could be better?"

"Hey, let's *go*!" they called out
and dashed over across the ground.

They rolled up, they rolled down,
they rolled over and all around!
Little brother followed
but made no sound.

One stopped and said, "What a ton of fun!
But wait…is *this* the very best one?"

19

All at once, a leaping lizard
caught their eye as it darted by.

"Will he lead us to better treasure?"
"Follow him! It's worth a try!"

20

"Who knows," they said, "which way we'll go!
We'll search up high, and we'll search down low!
We will not rest 'til we've found the best!"

21

"Look!" one yelled. "Is *that* our treasure?

See...a long and lumpy log!

Could it be? What could be better?"

22

"Okay let's *go*!" they called out
and dashed over across the ground.
They marched up, they marched down,
they marched over and all around!

One stopped and said, "What a ton of fun!
But how do we find the *very* best one?"

All at once, colorful clouds caught their eye as they drifted by.

"The Maker will lead us to better treasure!

Let's ask *Him*; He will reply!"

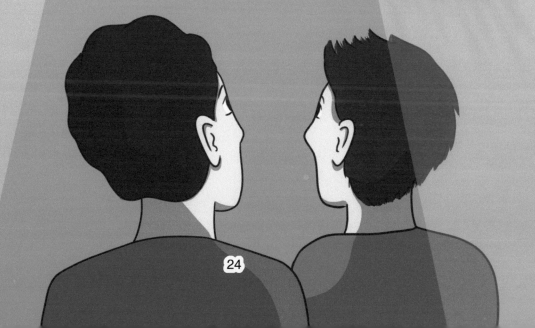

"He knows," they said, "which way to go!
He sees up high, and He sees down low!

Please hear our request
and show us the best!"

25

"Look!" they yelled.
"We can *spy* for treasure!
There…up those steep stairs!
Do we dare?
What could be better?"

"Woah, let's go!" they called out.
"Up to the top! We'll look all around!"
They climbed up, they climbed 'round,
they climbed high above the ground!

They stopped and said, "What a ton of fun!"

"Search everywhere! Find the *one*!"

All at once, a fancy feather
caught their eye as it blew on by.

"That is little brother's treasure!
Why is it here? Up in the sky?"

"*Look*," one cried, "on that treasure!
See…on our lumpy log!
Could it be? Could that be his sweater?"

31

"*Uh oh*…let's go!" they shouted out. "Little brother *must* be found!"
They ran down, they ran 'round, they ran right back to the ground!

They stopped and said, "This is not fun!
We've got to find that missing one!"

Now every little movement caught their eye as they darted by.
"Search for him like hidden treasure! Search everywhere, we've got to try!"

"*Lil bro*!" they cried. "Where did you go?
Please answer us! We're worried so!

We cannot rest,
Oh, what a mess!"

34

Two big brothers
raced past like a flash.

Straight for their brother,
they made a dash.

The brothers declared, both loud and clear,
"The best is what we asked to find.
Now we have the answer here…
We left the very best behind!"

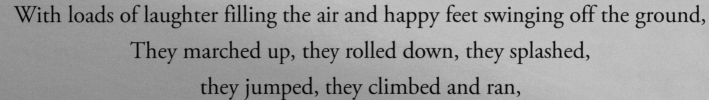

With loads of laughter filling the air and happy feet swinging off the ground,
They marched up, they rolled down, they splashed,
they jumped, they climbed and ran,
Up and over and all around…

38

Together!

About the Author

Catie lives in Colorado with her husband and their two Golden Retrievers. She enjoys hiking, biking, reading, writing, coaching and teaching. Growing up by the coast in California, the beach is always a favorite as well. Most of all, she loves spending time with family and friends. Her three boys are still the source of so much joy and seeing them choose to spend time together is a precious gift!

Printed in the USA
CPSIA information can be obtained
at www.ICGtesting.com
LVHW061018141124
796389LV00004BA/98